Decentralized Finance 2022-2023

Trading and investment strategies for beginners in cryptocurrency and NFTs

Edition 3.0

DEFI MEDIA HOUSE

&

STELLAR MOON PUBLISHING

Disclaimer

Profit from the bear market?

The bear market is often seen as a negative period, where investors mostly see their investment evaporate. Most people buy when the euphoria is highest, which in retrospect are often the least good buying times. This is precisely why the bear market is interesting. The euphoria is gone, but the opportunities are still there!

During this period you have the possibility to invest relatively cheaply and to put your time and energy in interesting developments, which most people are not occupied with at that moment. In this chapter you'll discover everything concerning the bear market, in which I'll take you along to several tips, so that during a bear market you'll be able to take optimal advantage of this difficult period!

What is a bear market?
In the traditional markets, a bear market is said to occur when a drop of 20% occurs. Experienced crypto investors laugh at these percentages, which can sometimes occur daily on the crypto market. A drop of 20% does not even bother many crypto investors, while the stock market, for example, would scream blue murder.

This makes it difficult to give an unequivocal answer to the question. In any case, you can speak of a bear market when the price is in a downward trend for an extended period of time and confidence in the market is very low. This pessimism is caused by the falling prices and the length of the bear market. In general, most investors are pessimistic about the future of crypto, so in this case they are bearish.

Sentiment during a bear market

A bear market is not the most euphoric period of your life. This can be clearly seen in the sentiment in cryptoland, where many investors are withdrawing or expressing themselves negatively via social media. Fear is growing among investors and more and more people are wondering if the market will recover. Out of fear, many investors are stepping out of the market, preferring to sell their crypto at their current loss rather than hold on to the investment any longer.

To take advantage of sentiment, it is useful to note your own emotions somewhere. This applies to the most bullish as well as the most bearish periods. If you later find yourself in a similar situation or recognize similar feelings, you can reflect on this on the basis of your earlier tremors. For example, do you have great fear after the price of Bitcoin capitulates? This has happened many times before, so you can better put the emotions and the price in perspective.

With these tips you will successfully pass the bear market!

During the bear market it is very easy to focus on something else. There are plenty of activities which are adventurous, enthusiastic or exciting during this period.

The crypto market, where the prices drop and the mood of many investors drops just as much, is when most people like to spend their time.

To make sure you can hold your own during this period, we have 7 tips that can help you maintain focus during this time. Using different investment strategies, you can discover which strategy is right for you and how to apply it!

1. Make a plan
The following tips contain specific activities which will help you to maximize your profits during a bear market. But the most important is this tip: make sure you always work with a plan. This will make your activities measurable and you'll be able to see how the progress is, and also where you might go wrong. In addition, it also prevents FOMO, because your plan serves as a guide.

In your plan, it is important to explain in detail how you are going to invest and what you will do with the returns. In doing so, it is also important that you think about the time frame. Both for the short and long term a plan is useful, but here a goal is also important. Ultimately, every investor has a motive, which caused that person to start investing.

2. Stopping your coins
It may happen that you missed the boat during a previous bull run and were not able to sell your coins in

time for a profit. When the price then makes a big drop, your investment is under water. In the very short term there is little chance that you will make a profit on these coins, but you can use them to expand your portfolio. By discontinuing your coins you ensure that you receive more crypto as a reward. Especially for the less risky crypto assets, like Bitcoin and most stablecoins, this can be a relatively safe way to expand your portfolio.

Another situation where crypto staking is useful is if you decide to invest for the long term. If you have bought your coins and you have decided to hold them for a longer period of time, then staking your coins is an interesting option. This allows you to increase your portfolio, in a way similar to saving on the savings account. You lock in your investment and receive a fee for it. However, the percentages in crypto are a lot higher! Where the bank only gives just 0.1% savings interest, with crypto you can strike quite easily with 10% as a reward.

3. Make money with NFTs in different ways!
Also with NFTs you can start making money in different ways. You can do this by buying and then owning NFTs, which will earn you coins if you own them. An example of this is the CyberKongz collection, where NFT holders receive 10 BANANA daily. This makes it possible to build passive income through NFTs. In addition, NFT cessation is an option to earn money online with non-fungible tokens.

Staking your NFTs is a relatively new way to put your unique token to work NFT staking means that you link your non-fungible tokens to a platform or protocol. In exchange for this action, you receive strike rewards. In this way, you can earn extra while remaining the owner of the NFT.

You can compare this method of staking to yield farming, where cryptocurrencies are lent or deployed to liquidity providers in order to earn rewards via interest or transaction fees. This way of earning interest is similar to that of a bank, but in this case there is no intermediary involved. NFT strike belongs to the decentralized financial world, while a bank is centralized.

4. Invest in Play-to-Earn gaming.
This tip is perhaps the most fun way to prepare for better crypto times! Through Play-to-Earn (P2E) gaming, you can provide some entertainment while earning crypto and NFTs in the meantime. In this way, you instantly ensure that a bear market doesn't have to be boring! The interest in cryptocurrencies decreases during a bear market and that also applies to these games. That's exactly why it's useful to build up a gaming portfolio during this period.

By investing in the right game, which after proper research you expect to flourish during a bull market, you can start playing P2E games. In your research, include how the team communicates, whether deadlines are met, what options the game has to offer and what blockchain the game is built on.

The blockchain may be important in relation to adoption. However, there are also very well-known games that are not built on Ethereum, for example. DeFi Kingdoms is an example of this, which is built on the Harmony blockchain, yet is incredibly popular with many gamers!

P2E games can often be played for free, but the most lucrative way is often to buy NFTs and deploy them. For some games this is mandatory, which is called NFT-to-earn. Regardless of what your strategy is with crypto games, on any blockchain you can find interesting games. From Crabada on Avalanche to Aavegotchi on Polygon!

5. Dollar Cost Average (DCA).
A common way to invest in blockchain technology is the Dollar Cost Average method (DCA method). Dollar Cost Averaging is seen as a useful strategy by many investors, including many crypto investors. In addition to crypto, this method of investing is also very useful for other markets, such as the stock, bond and commodity markets.

The feature of DCA is that an investor will invest at a fixed time for a certain amount. Also in which investment or even which coin you do this, you have predetermined. By making a plan before investing, you make sure that your emotions do not influence the investing. This can be very difficult in the volatile crypto market, so you can avoid unnecessary mistakes through the DCA method.

Also, this method of investing is very useful during a bear market. When your interest in investing in crypto is waning, you can turn on automatic investing and thus continue to invest silently, and be pleasantly surprised when your interest also rises again during a bull run.

6. Research different crypto projects
It is often the case that a bull market is relatively short, compared to bear markets. Because bear markets are often long, you can use the time during a bear market to do good research on different crypto projects. You can use this time to research which Crypto Pearls are going to make it all the way during the next bull run!

Especially during this period, researching projects is so important, because you can actually invest cheaply during this time. For example, investors who researched the different forms of crypto adoption in 2018 through 2020 could have tied this information to different niches. From CryptoPunks, play-to-earn gaming and crypto projects that compete with Ethereum; investors who used the previous bear market well were able to reap the benefits in the years that followed.

Here, not only are existing projects of interest, but new crypto projects can also be very interesting. However, often the plans consist of a nice website and a white paper, crypto start-ups are often a very risky investment, but high risk can also mean high reward.

7. Pay close attention to BTC pairing.
When Bitcoin starts a new bull run, it is important to get in position well with the right altcoins. In addition to doing a lot of research and having a good spread between risky coins and less risky coins, you can also keep an eye on the BTC pairing of an altcoin.

If all altcoins have fallen rock-hard in dollar value, but some coins have fallen a lot less hard in BTC value, this could potentially create opportunities. When Bitcoin rises, these coins can also rise very hard. The dollar value gives a distorted picture in these cases. However, by far most investors only look at the dollar value, but not at the BTC pairing.

But what is the BTC pairing? You've probably looked up the Bitcoin chart, where Bitcoin is pitted against the U.S. dollar or the euro. In this case, you speak of BTCUSD or BTCEUR as a pair. When looking for altcoins that are in better shape than the dollar value suggests, in the case of Polkadot for example, you search for DOTBTC, instead of DOTUSD.

The bear market is the most boring period of the market. There is no euphoria, fewer and fewer people are talking about the market and the sociability has been replaced by whining and negativity. Especially during this time, it is important to keep your mind on the matter, because these are the times when you can invest favorably. However, investing should always be done with a plan and proper research!

The above tips are meant to show that in a bear market you can make profits or expand your portfolio in different ways, so that you are optimally prepared when the price goes up again. You can make use of several tips, but especially for novice crypto enthusiasts, it is wise not to get involved with too many different things. Overview is important, which is very hard to find in the wild west of the blockchain industry.

Table of Contents

Your FREE Book

If you want to make a profitable start in the world of cryptocurrency, make sure to download our free bonus with **12 extremely valuable tips for beginners!**

With this book and these tips, you're guaranteed to make a great start with your future investments!

Sign up here to get instant access and kickstart your crypto success:

https://campsite.bio/stellarmoonpublishing

Are you looking for a new way to invest?

Are you looking to make some money?

Interested in investing but do not know where to start?

Do you want to start your crypto trading with the knowledge of reputable experts in finance and investment?

The crypto Expert Trading Course is the most comprehensive course on trading and investing with cryptocurrencies. You will learn how to trade in just a few minutes per day. We teach you everything from technical analysis, risk management, and much more.

Our goal is to help you become a successful trader so that your financial future can be secure.

Investing has never been easier with our step-by-step blueprint that teaches beginners how to trade like an expert – with the potential of making huge profits!

The best part about this course is taught by experts. So, what are you waiting for? Start today!

For more information, visit this link:

https://payhip.com/b/ork8N

Our books

Check out our other book to learn more about NFTs, NFT trading and selling, how to make profit and essential tips and strategies for a fail-proof start in the NFT universe.

Join the exclusive Stellar Moon Publishing Circle, you'll get instant access to **12 Extremely Valuable Crypto Tips**!

Besides that, you'll also get instant access to our mailing list with updates from our experts every week!

Sign up here today:

https://campsite.bio/stellarmoonpublishing

Dollar cost average (DCA)?

When trading crypto, it is often important to follow a strategy. A strategy ensures that you keep yourself to a plan that you have determined beforehand. This makes it easier to deal with unexpected situations, emotions and price fluctuations.

What such a strategy looks like, can of course be decided by everyone. There are plenty of crypto traders who come up with their own strategy that works best for them. It is also possible to use a strategy that has already been thought up by someone. One strategy you might come across then is Dollar Cost Averaging.

Dollar Cost Averaging, abbreviated as DCA, is an investment strategy that can be used by all kinds of traders. This strategy can make investing in crypto and other financial products a lot easier. You can read below what Dollar Cost Averaging is, how it works and by whom this strategy can be used best.

What is Dollar Cost Averaging (DCA)?
Dollar Cost Averaging is an investment strategy used by a large number of crypto traders. By the way, not only by crypto traders. Dollar Cost Averaging is in fact an incredibly old technique used by all kinds of investors. You can also use this tactic when you want to invest in stocks, bonds, ETFs, precious metals, etc.

Dollar Cost Averaging is all about investing a predetermined amount at a fixed time. You do this in a predetermined investment product. This way of investing ensures that you are not influenced by emotions, price rises and falls.

The idea behind Dollar Cost Averaging is that the price will gradually increase over a long period of time. You buy crypto at different times: during times when the price is low and during times when the price is high. By investing at different times, the amount of money you have invested will be the average of all these different buying times.

When is the best time to buy?
Dollar Cost Averaging is a strategy that you apply for the long term (at least a few years). You can decide how often you set a buying moment. In many cases people use Dollar Cost Averaging by investing monthly or quarterly.

Choosing a product in advance
It is important to choose a product to invest in beforehand, and not to abandon it. The idea behind Dollar Cost Averaging is that you invest part of your capital in the same product over a long period of time, so that you will have paid the average purchase price.

Example of DCA
Tim would like to invest his money in crypto, because he believes that this way it can become worth more

than if it were in his bank account. However, he has no knowledge about cryptocurrency. Therefore, he decides to invest 150 dollars in Bitcoin every month. After all, he can easily spare 150 dollars even if he loses it, and Bitcoin is the largest and most widely used cryptocurrency.

Therefore, this cryptocurrency seems the safest for him.

On the 25th of the month, his salary is deposited into the bank account. He therefore chooses to have 150 dollars automatically debited on the 26th of the month, so that he cannot spend the money in advance. This money is then used to automatically buy Bitcoin.

After a year, Tim has bought Bitcoin 12 times for the following prices:

January - 30,000
February - 28,000
March - 21,000
April - 22,000
May - 26,000
June - 31,000
July - 39.000
August - 40.000
September - 38.000
October - 55,000
November - 61,000
December - 64.000

The average price Pim paid is 37,916. When Pim decides to sell his Bitcoins after 12 months, he has made an average return of 68.8% on his investment, without having any knowledge about crypto or spending time gaining knowledge or conducting research.

Who is DCA suitable for?

Anyone can take advantage of Dollar Cost Averaging. There are several situations in which Dollar Cost Averaging may be wise. Consider the following situations:

Novice investor with no knowledge.
People who have little or no knowledge about investing, often find it difficult to determine buying and selling moments. However, they would like to take advantage of the potential returns. That is why DCA is a popular strategy among novice investors.

Investor without time.
If you do have the knowledge, but simply do not have the time to research new assets and the best moments to buy and sell, DCA can be a suitable strategy for you. You do not have to waste time when you use Dollar Cost Averaging.

Investor who wants to spread out. You can reduce the risk of losing money by not putting your money on one horse. This also applies to strategies that you follow. When you use different strategies, you reduce the risk of losing money when one strategy doesn't seem to be working.

Often we see that novice investors use DCA. This is because they do not yet have enough knowledge to do research on certain assets. In some cases, they also don't have the time, but are still eager to take advantage of the returns they can achieve.

Also, many experienced crypto traders choose to use Dollar Cost Averaging. This is because the strategy can be used as a portfolio diversification. By using different strategies, you reduce the risk of losing wealth. Should one strategy not work, you can always fall back on the other strategy.

How to use Dollar Cost Averaging in crypto trading? A step-by-step plan!
You now know what Dollar Cost Averaging is and why it can be so useful to use it. You might still have some questions about this strategy, the next one of which might be: how can you use Dollar Cost Averaging in crypto trading?

I'll explain what you need to do before you can start buying crypto according to DCA, after which I'll tell you on which platforms you can best use Dollar Cost Averaging.

Preparation

Decide how often you want to invest. Most people choose to make an investment monthly. We also see people who do this quarterly. Make sure it doesn't go beyond a quarter, or the idea behind spreading will be lost.

Decide how much money you want to invest. Of course, everyone can invest a different amount. Therefore, take a good look at how much money you can invest on a monthly/quarterly basis. Keep in mind that you can lose the money. Therefore, do not invest money that you actually cannot miss.

Decide which cryptocurrency you want to buy. It is important to choose a cryptocurrency that you have long-term confidence in. Many people choose Bitcoin (BTC) or Ethereum (ETH) because these are established blockchains and cryptocurrencies. Based on market capitalization, these are the two largest cryptocurrencies in the world.

Determine how you will execute DCA. You can execute DCA in two different ways:

- Manual investing. This involves making the purchases manually.
- Automatic investing. This means that a platform will automatically make the purchases for you.

At which crypto exchanges/brokers can you execute DCA automatically?

A number of crypto exchanges and brokers give you the opportunity to set up automatic purchases. You then indicate at what frequency you want a certain cryptocurrency to be purchased automatically.

Bitvavo.
On the platform of Bitvavo you cannot use a special DCA function, but it is possible to have money transferred automatically. You can read more about it here.

Coinmerce.
The crypto broker Coinmerce offers you the possibility to set up repetitive orders.

Binance.
You can also place a repeating order at Binance to apply DCA. Here you can read how to do that.

The biggest advantage is that you don't have to spend time buying DCA yourself when you have it done automatically by the crypto exchange/broker you use.

The advantages and disadvantages of DCA
Below you can read the important advantages and disadvantages of Dollar Cost Averaging (DCA).

Advantages

Trading without emotions.

When you always buy a certain asset at the same time, you will not be influenced by emotions, so you will be less at risk.

Easy to use.
It is not difficult to apply DCA.
Many exchanges and brokers even offer the option to set it up, so you don't have to manually purchase an asset.

No time or knowledge required.
Applying DCA allows you to invest in crypto, stocks or other products without having to invest time in doing research on these assets.

It is also not necessary to have a lot of knowledge beforehand, because with DCA you do not need that.
Stable increase over the long term.
When you use DCA, there is a good chance that the value of your investment will increase steadily over the long term.

Disadvantages

No guarantee of positive returns.
Despite the fact that DCA is a popular strategy and many people indicate that they earn a positive return as a result, it is of course no guarantee of achieving a profit. Therefore, keep in mind that you can also lose money with DCA.

Lesser profits.
If you use DCA as a strategy, you also buy an asset at times when the price is high.

As a result, in the short term you will make less profit than when you buy an asset when the price is as low as possible.

Dollar Cost Averaging is a popular strategy among crypto traders. However, the strategy is not being used for the first time within the crypto market. Dollar Cost Averaging is also a popular form of investment among traders of stocks, bonds and precious metals.

Dollar Cost Averaging involves investing a fixed amount of money in a particular asset at predetermined times. In the case of cryptocurrency, it would mean, for example, that you invest 100 euros in Bitcoin every 25th of the month. In this way, you always pay the average price and are not affected by emotions and price fluctuations.

DCA can be used by people who do not have time to do research on an asset. But also many advanced traders are a fan of Dollar Cost Averaging. This is because it also serves as a diversification tool. By spreading across different strategies, you run a lower risk of losing stakes.

Market Reflexivity

Market reflexivity is a term from sociology that is also widely used in the economic world. The definition is closely related to price levels and market sentiment. George Soros is a big name in the field of reflexivity theory, so that's why we cover his opinion in this chapter as well. By educating yourself on financial matters, you can benefit. After all, technical analysis and understanding the fundamental basics is the foundation of being a good trader.

In the second half of the chapter I will tell you what reflexivity has to do with the crypto market, so do read along? Oh yeah, just a heads up: always think carefully about your own investments and decisions, because I don't give financial advice. Do not blindly follow others and rely on your own findings, theories and experiences. Also, don't put in money you can't afford to lose, even if the market seems to be in such good shape. In this chapter you will learn why it is not wise to blindly follow the price increases...

What does Market Reflexivity mean?
Market Reflexivity is the same as market reflexivity. It is a term that originated in sociology, but is also relevant in the economic world. In the financial world, George Soros is a preacher of this term, so let's first dive into who he actually is and why his views are important to the financial market. And, of course, the crypto market in particular!

Who is George Soros?

George Soros is an American businessman and well-known philanthropist. He was inspired by Karl Popper (1957), who wrote the book "The Poverty of Historicism. With a net worth of almost $9 billion, he is very wealthy, although he donates much of his wealth to charities. The best man became known as 'the man who broke the bank of England' and is still known as a legend in the world of investments. He is also known for his book "The alchemy of Finance", which he wrote in 1987 but reissued a few years ago.

On September 16, 1992, he single-handedly destroyed the Bank of England. The gist of the story is that he took advantage of the European Monetary System while carrying out a speculative attack. At the time, there was devaluation in the economy (intentional depreciation of one currency against another). Soros figured that a major speculative attack would force the country to leave the system and devalue the currency.

George Soros vs. Market Reflexivity

But what does George have to do with Market Reflexivity? Economic theories, according to Soros, are invalidated by reflexivity. He believes that while market prices should strive for equilibrium, reflexivity ensures that this does not happen, or:

In situations that have thinking participants, the participants' view of the world is always partial and distorted...These distorted views can influence the situation to which they relate because false views lead to inappropriate actions. ...It's generally recognized that the complexity of the world in which we live exceeds our capacity to comprehend it. Confronted by a reality of extreme complexity we are obliged to resort to various methods of simplification.

So basically what it comes down to is that what our individual reality is does not correspond at all to what the real reality is. We all have our own unique view of the world and because of this we never 100% see the real objective situation. This also means, therefore, that investors take action based on their own perceptions, thus influencing reality. This reality includes the direction of the market. Through the perception of investors, they themselves are also influenced. Peculiar isn't it?

According to Soros, these actions and reactions land us in a feedback loop, which disconnects market prices and events from reality.

Deep dive into reflexivity
So, as described above, reflexivity theory is about the fact that investors make their decisions not based on reality, but on their perception of reality. Thus, they frame their reality, make a decision, and perform actions. From these actions flow perceptions, which have an impact on reality. As a result, prices in the

market change, which in turn changes reality in the eyes of investors.

According to George Soros, this process is self-reinforcing and is the cause of imbalanced prices in the market. According to the investor, the current economic situation is a textbook example of the theory: rising house prices lead to an increase in the number of mortgages, which in turn leads to a rise in prices. As a result, we massively form one bubble after another until it collapses. You can guess the result: a financial crisis, like the Great Recession between 2007 and 2009.

Although the standard assumption is an economic equilibrium combined with a rational expectation, Soros contradicts this. An equilibrium price, according to most economic models, comes about through supply and demand. According to the average economist, when demand is rationally expected to fall, the price decreases. Conversely, the price rises when demand increases or when there is scarcity.

George Soros does not fully agree with this, believing that reflexivity disturbs this equilibrium. Price development never stands still, and if we continue to make decisions based on what we consider to be our reality, then an ever-widening gap is created between reality and the level of market prices. The feedback loop mentioned earlier causes a discrepancy between prices and expectations. When something changes in the economy, a positive adjustment takes place through the feedback loop. A negative feedback loop would keep the market in equilibrium, but the normal reaction fails to occur. As a result, economic equilibrium disappears until market participants wake up and see that reality has become disconnected from market prices. The trend then temporarily reverses, but George Soros does not consider this a negative feedback loop.

Reflexivity in the crypto market
OK, we have now laid out quite a broad foundation of the concept, but what does this have to do with the crypto scene? Crypto is still young, so there are still violent fluctuations in the market: the so-called volatility. On top of that, as crypto-enthusiasts we constantly suffer from FOMO and always discover a new gem somewhere, am I right?

It is often portrayed in the news as if the entire crypto market depends on developments around Bitcoin (BTC), but if you have a little knowledge, you know that this is pure ignorance. As the market matures, the approach will grow along with that maturity. Because the market is so young, it is subject to fluctuations rather quickly. The fluctuations are caused by events in the market, which cause crypto to react negatively or positively.

Developments around Bitcoin
The fact that Bitcoin (BTC) is considered a financial revolution has a great impact on its reflexivity. Expressions such as "Bitcoin is unstable and will never make it as a serious means of payment" also affect the

market. Indeed, both of these are not factual matters, but sentimental events. In fact, these statements have a major impact on the price action surrounding the coin. Are we massively in favor of Bitcoin because the coin is making a jump and is in the news positively? Then the popularity rises and so does the price. If the price collapses, as it is at the time of writing (May 2022), then many people sell and it goes away for the proverbial dime.

Bitcoin's price development is relevant to the entire crypto market, as it is an influential asset. Of course, this is mainly because the market is young and many people hardly know anything about the market and its possibilities. In doing so, altcoins often follow Bitcoin's price, making it basically a self-fulfilling prophecy. For example, many people also predicted that the price of Bitcoin would rise to $200,000 by the end of 2021, which as we know did not happen. Worse, we've dipped quite a bit.

Bitcoin & the feedback loop
Judging by the price shifts over the last few years, you can very well see how Market Reflexivity works in practice. In 2020 and 2021, there was an incredibly bull market, meaning that the price was rising and higher than normal. Things were going incredibly well in the crypto market until Elon Musk announced that Bitcoin was no longer accepted as a means of payment at Tesla. In addition, mining was no longer allowed in China, which changed the sentiment on the market.

Prices fell and tensions prevailed on the crypto market. The panic caused many people to put their coins on sale. This led to even more panic last year, causing us to sink to an all-time low. Currently, Bitcoin (BTC) has dropped to 27k, leaving many investors waiting for another price rise and some perspective on the market. So you see, a reflexive market is fickle and exciting, which has far reaching consequences for consumers.

By the way, another thing that is affecting the price of Bitcoin is its heavily inflated value and the fact that people have come to see Bitcoin as a Store of Value (SoV). It is also called "the digital gold" because of the value that owners hold. The relationship between the two perceptions causes the price to be pushed up, causing reflexivity.

Despite the fact that reflexivity is fundamentally a sociological term, we hold the term against the economic market in this chapter. What does the relationship between cause and effect have to do with the financial market and how does price adjust to these fluctuations?

In a nutshell, reflexivity is the self-reinforcing effect of market sentiment, causing prices to tighten due to investor perception, until the process becomes unsustainable. George Soros is a big name who is widely associated with this definition. He gives a good example based on the current housing market. House prices rise

> more houses are sold and mortgage loans made > prices rise even further > it gets out of control and becomes unaffordable. The market price is no longer in proportion to the intrinsic value, so the market collapses.

Cryptocurrency volatility

Crypto and forex, they are two popular markets in which to trade. One trades digital currencies, while the other trades real life currencies like the euro or the yen.

Both markets have their advantages and their disadvantages. In general, for example, the crypto market is clearly more volatile than the forex market. Volatility means by how much the market moves up and up within a given time. Is this an advantage or a disadvantage? You can only determine that for yourself.

For some, it may be an advantage because more volatility potentially offers greater returns. On the other hand, high volatility also brings more risk.

How exactly is it that this volatility is higher and what should you take into account? You can read all that and more in this chapter.

What is the crypto market?
A cryptocurrency is a digital unit that represents a certain value. It is a digital currency used as an alternative to the money we are used to.

Crypto was once created after Satoshi Nakamoto tried to develop a peer-to-peer electronic cash system. This would make double spending of the same money impossible. Originally, it was not his intention that a cryptocurrency would emerge from this.

An important requirement for cryptocurrencies is that they do not require a server or a central authority and are therefore decentralized.

Many of these decentralized cryptocurrency networks are based on blockchain technology. This is a kind of ledger that is kept by an independent network of computers. This makes it impossible, for example, for money to be issued twice or for other forms of fraud to occur.

The crypto market is, of course, the place where cryptocurrencies can be bought and sold. It is the place where the demand for cryptocurrencies and the supply of cryptocurrencies meet.

What is the forex market?
The forex market is where currencies are traded. These are currencies like the euro, the dollar or the yen. These currencies are still very important today, because they are the ones that are generally used to pay all over the world.

The "price" of these currencies is determined by a lot of factors. Simply put, of course, as with anything, they are influenced by supply and demand. But how exactly does this form of supply and demand work?

For example, the demand for a currency increases when producers in the country of the currency become cheaper. Suppose prices in Europe fall. American companies can then buy products cheaper in Europe than in America. However, they have to do this in euros. As a result, they demand euros and the 'price', or exchange rate, of the euro rises.

So in the example mentioned earlier, the supply to dollars increases, because the United States offers these dollars in exchange for euros. The price of the dollar will therefore fall.

The fluctuations that thus take place in these prices, or rates, are very attractive to currency speculators. Currency speculators are people who speculate on the price of the currency. This means that they are likely to buy when they expect a price increase and to sell when they expect a price decrease.

Also in forex, just like in crypto or in stocks, there is a lot of money to be made. However, things can also go badly wrong. Take this into account before you start and always keep in mind: first learn and only then invest!

What are the differences between the crypto market and the forex market?
Now that we have discussed both markets, you might already have a bit of an image of what the differences are between the crypto market and the forex market. Nevertheless they resemble each other, after all on both markets you buy and sell currencies. On the one

you buy digital currencies and on the other non-digital currencies. But what exactly are the big differences between the two?

Market characteristics
One of the differences between the crypto market and the forex market is that the markets are not always open at the same time.

In fact, the forex market operates on weekends. It is actually and combination between the crypto market and the stock market. The stock market is in fact open 5 days of the week, on these open days the market is open for limited hours. The crypto market is open 24 hours a day, 7 days a week. So the forex market is an intervention of this. It is open 5 days a week, but 24 hours.

Volatility
In general, the crypto market is many times more volatile than the forex market. This means that there are many more price fluctuations in the crypto market than in the forex market.

This is due to several reasons. For example, it is because the crypto market is newer than the forex market. Later on we will go into how this works exactly and what the other reasons are.

Risk

Of course, you can never say which market is riskier. It so happens that this depends on so many different factors and next to that the risk is also to a great extent dependent on your actions.

In general, the risk on the forex market is a bit smaller than the risk on the crypto market. The main reason for this is simply that the forex market is less volatile. Consequently, less enormous fluctuations take place in the prices, as a result of which you'll run somewhat less risk to suddenly lose a lot of money. Of course, the chance to suddenly earn a lot of money is also a bit smaller.

Of course, you can also reduce or increase the risk as a consequence of your choices. Always pay attention and always do your research first. Always remember the well-known rule: learn first and invest later!

Centralization
Another huge difference between the two markets is that one is centralized and the other decentralized.

Forex, in fact, is centralized. This means that the currencies are controlled and dominated by central governments or banks. They decide what happens to the currency and can therefore influence its price.

Crypto is decentralized. This means that actually exactly the opposite takes place than what happens with forex.

Crypto is in fact not dominated or controlled by anyone. According to many, this is a great advantage.

Term
Trading in forex is mainly for the short term. This is because if you as a Dutch speculator for instance buy the rand (currency of South Africa), you won't have any further use for it. Your only goal as a speculator when buying this currency is to make a profit.

With crypto, this does not have to be the case in all cases. Some crypto currencies have a real project behind them, with a special advanced technology that could actually change the world. With crypto, therefore, there is a good chance that you may be purchasing the crypto for the sake of the project and its function, beyond the goal of just making a profit.

This is a big difference, the impact of which can be clearly seen in both markets.

Location Binding
Both investments are location dependent to some extent.

For forex this is very easy to explain. This is because the currency you buy or sell belongs to a location or multiple locations. For example, the dollar belongs to the United States and the euro belongs to all of Europe.

In the early days of crypto, you couldn't really say that crypto was location bound and maybe it still isn't. However, there are a few caveats to this. Crypto, or certain crypto projects specifically, are now banned in some places in the world. You also have techniques that only work or are active in certain countries. Thus, also crypto is to some extent location bound. In the future this could become more or less the case.

Market cap
There are also differences in the total market cap of the two markets. This means how big the total market is in its entirety.

The market cap of forex is the biggest of any market. The forex market is therefore the largest market there is in the entire world. The total market cap of forex is $5,000,000,000,000. The USD (United States Dollar) is the biggest player in this. This currency namely accounts for 90% of the total market.

The total market cap of crypto is considerably smaller. It is approximately $300,000,000,000. Bitcoin (BTC) is the largest player and accounts for approximately half of this market cap. In second place is Ethereum (ETH), which accounts for about 8% of the entire crypto market cap. These figures apply in the year 2021.

Why is the crypto market more volatile than the forex market?

When you make a choice about which market you want to start trading in, it's important that you take all aspects of both markets into account, including the volatility. The volatility implies the size of the fluctuations in the prices. In other words, how much do these prices move up and down.

It's important to know this about the market in which you're going to trade, because this way you'll be able to determine well how you're going to trade. The risk you're going to take, depends on the volatility.

The higher the volatility, the higher in general the risk. This is because when the volatility is higher, in principle the chance is bigger that the market suddenly drops and so does your investment. If you want to take this risk then of course you can, but it is important that you make a good consideration in this.

In general the crypto market is more volatile than the forex market. This has several causes.

One of them is the size of the market. As already discussed earlier in this chapter, the crypto market is many times smaller than the forex market. A simple reasoning for this is that the crypto market is relatively new and also not yet "accepted" by everyone. On the other hand, the forex market is used by everyone, whether they want to or not. After all, everyone has to use currencies traded on the forex market in some way.

The consequence of this difference in size is than a transaction of a certain amount has more influence on the crypto market than on the forex market. When, for example, suddenly $3 million worth of crypto is sold, this is 1% of the total market and consequently the supply will increase with a much larger part than in the same transaction on the forex market. This will also cause the price to drop much more.

This also means, for example, that big players can exert much more influence on the market. For example, a tweet from Elon Musk would have much, much more influence on the crypto market than on the forex market.

In particular, the differences in size and age of the market ensure that the volatility on the crypto market is much higher than on the forex market.

So why is it that the crypto market is more volatile than the forex market? The main reasons for this are that the crypto market is many times smaller than the forex market and that the crypto market is a lot younger than the forex market. This together ensures that the crypto market is therefore more influenced by smaller transactions and, for example, more easily influenced by big players.

So why is this important? It's very important to keep the volatility of a market in mind before you start trading in it. Generally speaking, when the volatility is higher, the risk is also higher.

This is because in that case the risk is greater, as the market in principle moves back and forth more often and consequently also goes down more frequently. The chance of losing money is therefore greater.

DeFi Crimes

As more and more people become interested in the crypto world and more and more crypto tokens are traded, crypto crime is also on the rise. Criminals are everywhere these days in the crypto world, looking for new opportunities to take away people's assets.

The crypto world is changing rapidly, and so is crypto crime. New trends are visible every year. These can be completely new forms of crime, but also old forms in a new guise. In this blog you will read all about the latest crypto crime trends, so you can be extra alert and avoid becoming a victim.

Crypto crime figures
Crypto offers an alternative to the traditional financial sector through a decentralized system, which is independent of banks and the government. Transactions can be carried out quickly in a single network and are difficult to trace back to individuals. In addition to its many advantages, this method of trading also involves risks. Various parties are warning against the dangers of the crypto market and are asking for more supervision. Crypto-currencies are vulnerable to various forms of crime, because criminals have also found the crypto market. Especially the increasing popularity in connection with the anonymous and cross-border nature of crypto, offers opportunities for criminals.

In 2021, crypto related crime reached a new record, according to research by cryptanalysis company Chainalysis. A total of $14 billion in illegal transactions were received, compared to $7.8 billion in 2020, $11.7 billion in 2019, and $4.4 and $4.6 billion in 2018 and 2017, respectively. These were different types of illegal transactions.

However, these figures do not tell the whole story. The use of crypto is growing faster than ever, so more and more people are buying and selling crypto. Research shows that the total trading volume of crypto will have grown to $15.8 trillion by 2021. This is an increase of some 567% over the total trading volume in 2020. Given this growth, it is no surprise that more and more criminals are also using crypto to commit crime.

However, proportionally, the percentage of illegal crypto transactions has decreased when looking at previous years. In 2021, the percentage of illegal crypto transactions was 'only' 0.15% of the entire trading volume. In 2020 it was 0.62%, in 2019 as much as 3.37%, and in 2018 and 2017 the percentage was 0.76% and 1.42%. The share of illegal transactions in the total trading volume of crypto has never been as low as it is now. Therefore, the conclusion is that the legal use of crypto has actually increased.

Crime thus seems to occupy an increasingly smaller place within the crypto-ecosystem. On the one hand, this can be explained by the fact that crypto is taken more seriously by an increasing public as a digital payment or investment tool. Research by Ipsos, for example, shows that some 1.2 million Dutch people owned crypto in 2021. On the other hand, crypto has now also received more attention from governments, regulators and enforcers. Thus, the ability of law enforcement agencies to fight crypto-based crime is also evolving.

Of course, despite the percentage of illegal transaction has decreased, $14 billion in illegal activity is still a lot of money and is therefore problematic. Criminal abuse of crypto creates huge barriers to further developments and integrations, increases the likelihood of severe restrictions by the government, and worst of all, innocent people fall victim to this and lose a lot of money.

It is therefore good to dwell on the crypto crime trends, so that you can at least be alert to them.

Trends in crypto crime
What trends are visible in crypto crime? The table below gives the percentages of different types of crime in recent years. Looking at these percentages, two categories increased a lot in percentage terms in 2021: theft of crypto and to a lesser extent scams.

DeFi
In both stealing crypto and scams, DeFi plays a big role. What is DeFi? Decentralized Finance, abbreviated as

DeFi, literally means decentralized finance. DeFi is a development that makes it possible to provide financial instruments and services without depending on an intermediary such as a bank. This is done through smart contracts on the blockchain, which process financial transactions without intermediaries.

Scams

Revenue from scams increased 82% to $7.8 billion in stolen crypto from victims in 2021. More than 2.8 billion of this amount was obtained through back pulls. Back pulls represent a fairly new type of scam, where scammers pretend to be trustworthy and then pull all the money out of the project. This goes beyond just stealing crypto, there really has to be deception and gaining the trust of investors. In many cases, these were DeFi projects, where scammers tricked investors into buying tokens belonging to a particular project and then making off with the investors' money. The tokens are then worth nothing.

A well-known example of a back pull is the Squid game back pull, which took place in November 2021. Squid Game (SQUID) was a project based on the popular Netflix series and was supposed to be a play-to-earn game on the Binance Smart Chain, according to the white paper, but the game never came to fruition in the end. After the token reached a value of $2.86 after a rapid rise of 7400%, the creators pulled the money out and the token plummeted to as good as $0. Investors were left empty-handed. It is estimated that the scammers made between $3 million and $12 million.

Back pulls are common within DeFi for several reasons. First, it is because of the hype surrounding DeFi. In fact, the trading volume of DeFi projects increased by 912% in 2021. The high return on decentralized tokens has made many excited to invest in DeFi tokens. At the same time, it is not very complicated to create new DeFi tokens and place them on exchanges, even without a code audit. A code audit is a process by which an outside company or exchange analyzes the smart contract code behind a new token or other DeFi project. The external company then publicly confirms that the rules of the contract are reliable, and thus do not contain a mechanism for developers to get away with investors' crypto. You can therefore avoid becoming a victim of a back pull by only investing in projects that have undergone a code audit.

Crypto theft

Theft of crypto grew even more than scams. About $3.2 billion worth of crypto was stolen in 2021; this represents an increase of some 516% compared to 2020. About 2.2 billion of that, 72% of the 2021 total, was stolen from DeFi protocols. DeFi theft can be traced to errors in the smart contracts, making it possible for hackers to steal crypto. This increase in DeFi-related theft is in line with the trend that is visible that DeFi has become a major factor in crypto crime.

In 2020, just under $162 million worth of crypto was stolen from DeFi platforms. That was 31% of the total crypto stolen for the year. That alone then amounted to a 335% increase over 2019. In 2021, that percentage increased by another 1330%. In other words, as DeFi has continued to grow, so has the problem of crypto theft within Defi.

Money Laundering

There has also been growth in the use of DeFi for money laundering. In 2021, an increase of some 1964% was visible in this. This is also not very surprising. After all, criminals who scam people and steal crypto ultimately have one goal: to keep this stolen crypto hidden from the authorities and convert it into legal money so that it can be spent without proving its illegal origin. Money laundering therefore underlies all forms of crime with crypto, but because the popularity of DeFi has skyrocketed and offers many opportunities, criminals see many opportunities there as well.

NFTs

NFTs were one of the biggest hypes in 2021. As is the case with any new form of technology, NFTs offer many opportunities for abuse. On the one hand, NFTs are used as a tool for crypto theft or scams. Common NFT scams include fake NFT projects, copycat NFTs or NFT hacks.

On the other hand, NFTs are also bought with crypto obtained in an illegal way. As with physical art, NFTs can easily be used for money laundering. As shown in the graph below, the value of illegally obtained crypto sent to NFT marketplaces increased significantly in 2021.

The use of crypto is growing faster than ever and thus more and more people are trading with crypto. Due to this growth, crypto crime is also increasing. We can clearly see that DeFi plays an important role in this. DeFi offers huge opportunities for companies and investors, but it also offers opportunities for criminals and new forms of crime. So be warned and do not invest in projects without first doing proper research on the reliability and intentions behind the project!

Defi insurances

I probably don't need to tell you that trading crypto is risky. When you buy crypto, the value can go up, but it can just as easily go down. So you are always at risk of losing stakes. That's just part of crypto trading.

Yet you can also lose money in very different ways within the crypto world. Think not only of scams and scam coins, but also of technical errors. Those kinds of errors are quite common within DeFi.

Fortunately, more and more companies are looking for solutions to these kinds of errors. For example, consider special DeFi insurances. These types of DeFi insurances are becoming increasingly popular. Nexus Mutual, NSure Network and Ease are some of those kinds of insurances.

The Risks of DeFi
When you use DeFi, there are a number of risks around the corner. This is because DeFi relies on smart contracts. These are automated scripts that run on the blockchain. Such smart contracts process large amounts of cryptocurrencies, or in some cases hold them.

The moment something goes wrong within a smart contract, no one can fix the problem. This is because everything happens completely automatically and is recorded directly on the blockchain. Transactions are irreversible, so a mistake cannot be reversed.

When you use a DeFi protocol, you always have to take into account the loss of money due to errors in a smart contract. And should you lose money, that is of course very disappointing. There is nothing you can do about it, except not using the platform.

Fortunately, there are solutions for this kind of risk. Several companies have come up with a special insurance that can cover you against these kinds of losses.

What is a DeFi insurance?
DeFi insurance, or DeFi insurance, is insurance that covers you against the risks of DeFi. As you just read, using a DeFi protocol is not entirely without risk or danger. There is always a chance that something could go wrong, causing you to lose your bet.

DeFi insurances themselves run as dApp on the blockchain. In this way, it is possible to track hacks or errors on the blockchain. Some protocols have a built-in tool that can monitor hacks and errors. In this way, it is possible to determine exactly how much cryptocurrency you have lost.

Because such insurance policies run on the blockchain, there is no central party that can provide payment of claims. Instead, it is other people who take care of this. Of course, how exactly this is done and works varies from DeFi insurance.

Nexus Mutual (NXM)

Nexus Mutual is an application that runs on the Ethereum (ETH) blockchain. You could think of it as a decentralized insurance company. Yet, unlike central insurance companies, Nexus Mutual is not for profit. It is a mutual, which means the company is owned by the policyholders. All profits will be distributed among them.

By purchasing insurance from Nexus Mutual, you can protect yourself from code errors in DeFi applications. If you lose money during a token swap due to a UniSwap error, Nexus Mutual will compensate you for the loss.

How does Nexus Mutual work?

First, you specify on the Nexus Mutual website which protocol you want insurance for. You have a choice of many DeFi applications, such as Aave, Balancer or UniSwap. Next, you'll have to pay for the insurance, and you'll put down collateral. All payments from policyholders are kept in a pool.

The moment you have suffered a loss, you can make a claim. The network will then vote on the validity of the claim. Users who try to defraud are punished harshly: the collateral will be taken away. So it does not pay to try to cheat.

In the process, cheating is impossible. All events are stored on the blockchain, so one can always see what happened in the past. You cannot, as a loner, modify the history of the blockchain. You would have to own more than 51% of the network to do so, which is technically impossible in many cases.

The moment you have purchased insurance and make a valid claim, the protocol will cover the damage. The damage is covered from the pool. You will be sent the amount in the form of NXM tokens to your wallet address. You can then convert the tokens to other cryptocurrencies or to fiat currency.

You can cancel the insurance at any time. In that case, you will be refunded the collateral you have put in to your wallet address.

Nexus Mutual Exchange Custody Cover

You can also get insurance from Nexus Mutual against loss of crypto when a wallet or exchange is hacked. It is possible to make a claim once you have lost more than 10% of your holdings or are unable to make a transaction on the platform for more than 90 days.

It is possible to take out Custody Cover insurance for Celsius, BlockFi, Nexo, inLock, Ledn, Hodlnaut, Coinbase, Kraken and Gemini.

NXM token

Nexus Mutual has its own NXM token. You can use the token for strike to cover smart contracts. NXM has governance features and as an NXM token owner, you can also review claims for validity.

How can you use Nexus Mutual?
You can use Nexus Mutual by first navigating to the platform. You do that by clicking here. Next, you will need to connect your external crypto wallet, and then be able to select a protocol and insurance package. Next, go through the steps to purchase the insurance.

NSure Network
NSure Network is an open insurance platform for Open Finance. Chances are it doesn't mean much to you. You may have heard of Lloyd's London. This is a marketplace where insurance risks can be resold.

In such a marketplace, insurance issuers can resell policies. If you think that the risk of a claim is low, you could buy such an insurance policy. You will then receive the premium paid by the policyholder, but will also have to bear the possible costs.

Trading insurance can be lucrative, but it is also very risky. This is because it could cost you a lot of money should someone make a claim for their insurance. You are legally obligated to cover the claimed amount if you are the buyer of the policy.

How does NSure Network work?
NSure's decentralized protocol allows anyone to purchase insurance or cover risk for policyholders. As a

capital provider, you can see on the platform what kind of insurance people would like to have. Then you can decide to stake NSURE tokens on an insurance request that looks attractive. Such an application may be attractive if you expect the risk to be small. You will receive daily rewards in the form of NSURE tokens when you cover someone's risk.

Before you can do that, however, you will need to secure collateral. This way the protocol knows for sure that you would be able to cover a possible loss. Because should something go wrong, you as the lender will have to pay for the costs. So in effect, the risk is shifted from the user to the lender. The lender, however, can earn a nice return on the risk that is covered.

The cost you have to pay as a policyholder is determined by supply and demand. When a large number of people want to cover the risk of policyholders, the policyholders pay a lower price. This also means that the lenders will receive lower remuneration.

NSURE-token
NSure Network has an NSURE token. This token plays an important role within the protocol, as you just read. In addition, NSURE also has a governance function, and owners can have a say in the organization and future of the protocol. NSURE can of course also be used for price speculation.

How can you use NSure Network?
You can use NSure Network by first navigating to the platform. You do that by clicking here. Next, you will need to connect your external crypto wallet (choice of Metamask or Wallet Connect), and then be able to select a protocol and insurance package. Next, go through the steps to purchase the insurance.

Ease
Ease is a protocol where you can buy insurance against loss of money through DeFi protocols. This project was previously called ArmorFi, but changed its name and branding in early 2022. Users can protect themselves from hacks, scams and back pulls through Ease. According to Ease, they can do so in a way that is simpler, safer and more effective than many other insurance protocols do.

Other insurance protocols require you to lock in collateral. This collateral must be equal to the value of the tokens you are insuring. The moment the collateral decreases in value, or the covered tokens increase in value, you will have to take out a new insurance plan.

This ensures that this type of application can be used by only a small portion of crypto traders. This is because you need to be in possession of a large amount of money before you can insure yourself against the risks. Ease has come up with a solution called Uninsurance.

How does Uninsurance work?

Covering DeFi damages is what Ease does with Uninsurance. Previously, this solution was called Armor Smart Cover. All assets covered by the ecosystem immediately serve as collateral. As a result, participants do not need to put up additional collateral, and everyone can participate in Ease.

There will always be enough collateral. This is because the value of the covered assets is equal to the value of the total collateral. In this way, Ease aims to be an insurance protocol that makes itself as user-friendly as possible.

The moment a hack occurs, the victims' assets are immediately liquidated to make up for the loss.

You can participate in Uninsurance without having to pay for the services. This is because the assets of all participants directly serve as collateral, so there is no need to pay fees. You can cancel your insurance by removing your assets.

ARMOR token
The Ease ecosystem still uses the ARMOR token for governance functions. In the future, ARMOR will be converted to the EASE token. When this will happen is not yet known.

How can you use Ease?
You can use Ease by first navigating to the platform. You do that by clicking here. Next, you will need to connect

your external crypto wallet, and then be able to select a protocol and insurance package. Next, go through the steps to purchase the insurance.

Using a DeFi protocol or platform is not entirely without risk. There is always a chance of losing money. All DeFi products use smart contracts, and something can go wrong there. Because blockchain technology is irreversible and decentralized, mistakes cannot be fixed.

Fortunately, you can get insurance against this kind of risk from Nexus Mutual, NSure Network and Ease. With these types of protocols, you need to worry a little less about the risks, although it is important to still be aware of the risks you face at all times.

The safest stablecoin

Stablecoins seem simple, yet they come in all different shapes and sizes. Therefore, it can be difficult to choose which stablecoin is best to use.

Of course, you would prefer to use a stablecoin that is easy to use, but is one of the safest stable crypto coins in the world.

We're happy to tell you more about the most popular stablecoins you could use in this chapter. I'll also go into more detail about how each stablecoin is backed and what the security of the stablecoin is like.

What is a stablecoin?

Stablecoins are cryptocurrencies that always have a stable value. This value is linked to the price of another asset.

In most cases, it is a fiat currency. For example, the value of a stablecoin can always be equal to the euro or US dollar, which means that one stablecoin is also worth one euro or dollar.

A stablecoin must be backed by an underlying asset. In many cases it does not matter what the underlying asset is, as long as the total value equals the demand.

This is because supply and demand must be equal to ensure stability.

What stablecoins are there?

Today you have the choice of a large number of stablecoins. It can be difficult to make a choice from the large supply. Let alone knowing which stablecoin is the safest. Below we tell you what the most popular stablecoins are, how they work and in what way they are backed.

Tether (USDT)

Tether (USDT) is the most popular stablecoin in the world. This stablecoin has been one of the top 5 largest cryptocurrencies for years, based on market cap. Tether reflects the price of the US dollar, as do most other stablecoins.

Tether was launched by the eponymous company in 2014 as Realcoin. At the time, Tether ran on Bitcoin's blockchain in conjunction with the Omni platform. Not much later, Realcoin's name was changed to USTether, only to be changed back to USDT shortly after. As you probably also know, Tether is currently not only available on Bitcoin's blockchain. You can now trade this cryptocurrency on the blockchain of Ethereum, EOS, Algorand, OMG and TRON.

Is Tether safe?

In 2020, Tether made the news when it was revealed that most of the USDT tokens were backed by commercial bank money. It was at least 97% of the circulating coins.

Commercial bank money is money that does not physically exist, but can only be found as a number in a bank account. In many cases, commercial bank money is considered less secure, compared to cash. Tether then indicated to convert the commercial bank money to cash.

In the past, USDT once dropped to a value of $0.88, which is also the same as the ATL (all-time-low) of USDT.

Some people express concern about the security of Tether. Nevertheless, it has never gone wrong so far, and Tether indicates it will make itself even more secure in the future.

USD Coin (USDC).
The USD Coin (USDC) is pegged to the US dollar. Launched in 2018, this stablecoin is now available on more than 30 blockchains, including Solana's blockchain, Algorand, Binance Smart Chain and Fantom.

Circle and Coinbase are the companies behind the development of USD Coin. They created this stablecoin because they wanted to issue a secure stable crypto currency that is also easy to use. Therefore, they made the stablecoin available on a large number of blockchains.

Based on market cap, USD Coin is the second largest stablecoin in the world.

How secure is USD Coin?

So far, no major problems have been discovered with USD Coin. Back in 2020, the founders of USD Coin indicated that there would be a major update to the protocol and smart contracts of USD Coin. These updates were supposed to make the use of USDC easier. Users should be able to use USD Coin for daily payments without having to worry about security.

The value of USD Coin is backed by cash. The amount of cash USD Coin has in reserve is equal to the number of USDC coins issued. In this way, the stable value of USDC is guaranteed.

Binance USD (BUSD)

Crypto exchange Binance has issued a stablecoin together with Paxos which runs on the Binance Chain. Binance USD (BUSD) has been tradable since 2019 and has its value pegged to the US dollar. BUSD is issued as an ERC20 and BEP2 token, which means it can also be used on other blockchains, such as Ethereum.

Is Binance USD (BUSD) a secure stablecoin?

BUSD is approved by the New York State Department of Financial Services (NYDFS) and is also regulated by this organization. Every month The BUSD Monthly Audit Report is posted on the Binance website. In this report you can find developments of BUSD, such as the total number of issued stablecoins and how they are covered. Binance is therefore very transparent on BUSD and wants to ensure that people have confidence in it.

Paxos ensures that dollars are kept in reserve in order to guarantee a constant value. These reserves are held at a U.S. bank and by U.S. Treasuries.

So far, there have been no problems with the security of Binance USD. Meanwhile, BUSD is among one of the most popular stablecoins in the world.

Dai (DAI).
The blockchain of Ethereum is running DAI. This is a stablecoin that has the same value as the US dollar. However, the value is not covered by U.S. dollars. It is kept equal and covered by cryptocurrencies by means of the Maker Protocol and MakerDAO.

The Maker Protocol ensures that a number of cryptocurrencies are held in a smart contract. The value of these cryptocurrencies must be equal to the total number of DAI stablecoins issued. Therefore, the protocol is constantly buying and selling cryptocurrencies. This does not only take into account the number of stablecoins in circulation.

Of course, the value of the held cryptocurrencies can also change. Therefore, the protocol will have to ensure stability on several fronts.

Is DAI a secure stablecoin?
The value of DAI is covered by other cryptocurrencies.
An automated algorithm ensures that supply and
demand remain the same, giving DAI a constant value of
$1. Despite DAI working in a completely different way
than most stablecoins, no problems have been
discovered with DAI so far.

TerraUSD (UST)
TerraUSD (UST) is the stablecoin issued by Terraform
Labs. The value of this stablecoin is kept stable by Terra
(LUNA).

This is a protocol that ensured that UST is covered by
LUNA. Once the demand for UST increases, LUNA
owners are encouraged to exchange their LUNA for
UST. For this they receive more UST than LUNA, making
it financially attractive to swap tokens.

When the demand for UST decreases, UST owners are
encouraged to swap their UST for LUNA. In this way, the
coverage of UST is kept equal to the number of UST
tokens issued.

Is TerraUSD (UST) safe?
By mid-May 2022, it became clear that TerraUSD is not
a safe stablecoin. The value of stablecoin dropped, after
which many people decided to sell LUNA tokens. This
caused LUNA to fall. This drop was so fast that Terra's
protocol could not burn UST fast enough. The result:
both UST and LUNA dropped in value even faster.

On May 13, 2022, the team behind Terra even decided to pause the blockchain. They wanted to set up a plan of action before moving forward. It is not yet clear if it is going to succeed in getting TerraUSD working again. A bigger question is whether it will succeed in getting people to trust Terra and TerraUSD again.

TrueUSD (TUSD)
TrueUSD (TUSD) is a stablecoin issued by the company TrustToken. The value of TUSD is always pegged to the US dollar and is backed by dollars. All TUSD tokens are issued through a smart contract on TrustToken's platform. The company has several banks as partners that hold dollars for the number of tokens they have issued.

In 2019, TrueUSD became the world's first stablecoins to issue real-time audits. It is possible for anyone to see the status of TrueUSD on the TrustToken platform. This shows that TrustToken is thus open and transparent about TrueUSD.

Is TrueUSD (TUSD) a safe stablecoin?
Since its launch in 2018, TrueUSD has not experienced any problems. TrustToken has also been very open about TrueUSD's coverage so far. The stablecoin is fully backed by dollars, which are held in reserve by banks. On the platform of TrustToken, you can see how many dollars are in reserve, and thus know whether TrueUSD is sufficiently covered.

At the same time, TrueUSD is a lesser known stablecoin. Therefore, it might be wise to do some good research on this stablecoin yourself, before you decide to move your assets to this currency.

USDD (USDD)

USDD (USDD) is one of the newest stablecoins you will encounter in this chapter. This stablecoin was issued in May 2022 by the TRON DAO Reserve and runs on the TRON blockchain. TRON has built a mechanism into the stablecoin that ensures USDD can always keep itself stable. The value is pegged to the US dollar.

Is USDD safe?

The value of USDD is backed by the TRON DAO Reserve. This makes USDD the world's first stablecoin backed by a crypto reserve. Because USDD has only just launched, it is not clear at this point whether USDD is safe. It will take some time before we know if USDD contains any vulnerabilities, or if it is resistant to all kinds of attacks. Therefore, it doesn't hurt to be careful and do thorough research on USDD before you decide to purchase this stablecoin.

There are many different stablecoins available. Each stablecoin works in a different way, and is also backed in a different way. This can make certain stablecoins safer than other stablecoins. It is wise to always do your own research on how a stablecoin works, before you decide to have your assets protected by this stablecoin.

The mindset of investing

People are not as rational as we often think ourselves to be, and this is even more true when it comes to financial matters and uncertainties. Because the world is so complex, we are confronted with more information than we can consciously process. Our brains then make short-cuts, causing decisions to bypass our conscious thought process. This can lead to psychological thinking errors, which can ultimately result in making wrong decisions.

This chapter discusses key insights when making choices in uncertain times and discusses 10 common psychological thinking errors that can play a role when trading crypto or NFTs.

Decisions

Before we talk about decisions, it's good to first consider the concept of a decision. What exactly is a decision?

What is a decision?

In the book 'Rational Choice in an Uncertain World', Hastie & Dawes describe a decision as a response to a situation that consists of three different components:

First, there must be an uncertain situation.
Second, there must be at least two different choices.
Third, there must be positive and negative consequences associated with the choices.

Thus, a decision is a response to an uncertain situation, where there are multiple choices that can have both positive and negative consequences.

An example:
After lots of good stories from friends and information you've read on the Internet, you want to start investing in crypto in hopes of making a profit. You choose Bitcoin (BTC). Over the past few weeks, Bitcoin has only gone up. On the one hand, a correction could be coming by now, but on the other hand, Bitcoin is currently so bullish that the rise could also continue for a while. You are now faced with an important choice: do you buy crypto currencies now or wait a while?

If you buy crypto coins now, there are two consequences: the price rises further and you make a profit (positive) or the price falls and you make a loss (negative). On the other hand, you can also wait a while before buying crypto coins, but that also has consequences: the price rises further, making the crypto coins more expensive (negative) or the price falls, making the crypto coins cheaper (positive).

Making a decision is usually mainly about weighing the positive and negative consequences of the possible choices you have. Whether people choose to make a certain investment will therefore depend on the expectations of the price at that moment, the expected return and your attitude and knowledge of the risks involved in what you want to invest in.

The next question is how exactly to take such a decision.

How do we make decisions?

There are several theories that explain how we make decisions. In this chapter we discuss the dual process theory of Daniel Kahneman.

Daniel Kahneman is professor emeritus of psychology and public affairs at The Princeton School of Public and International Affairs at Princeton University. He is a major pioneer at the interface of psychology and economics, and in 2002 became the first psychologist to win the Nobel Prize in economics for integrating psychological insights with economic science, particularly with respect to human decision-making under uncertainty. Kahneman is therefore one of the most influential psychologists in the world and wrote the bestseller "Thinking, Fast and Slow" in 2011. In this book he demonstrates that humans are irrational beings, distinguishing two systems of thinking: fast thinking and slow thinking.

The dual process theory

Kahneman's dual process theory is a basic theory of decision making. According to this theory, we make decisions based on two cognitive systems:

System 1 Fast thinking: fast, automatic, unconscious.
System 2 Slow thinking: slow, deliberate, conscious.

According to Kahneman, we have two different systems of thinking. Fast thinking is an irrational, fast, intuitive way of thinking and slow thinking a rational, slow, deliberate way.

Both systems are very useful in practice, but we often arrive at incorrect decisions by using the wrong way of thinking, without being aware of it. When we rush to make a decision on a complicated issue, we do so through system 1. This can lead to psychological thinking errors, which can ultimately result in making wrong decisions. By using system 2 to make an informed decision, this can usually be avoided. However, Kahneman's book shows that when making important decisions, we often think we are using system 2, when in fact we are not. Our brains then make short-cuts to avoid wasting precious energy, causing decisions to bypass our conscious thought process. The conclusion is that we use system 1 much more often than we realize.

Heuristics and thinking errors
As just explained, hasty decisions using system 1 can lead to psychological thinking errors, causing us to make wrong decisions. The following explains exactly how this process works.

People are not as rational as we often lead ourselves to believe. A great deal of research has shown that calculating and rationally behaving people, homo economicus, are nothing but a myth. Because the world is so complex, we are confronted with more information than we can consciously process. This is even more true when it comes to financial matters and uncertainties.

It starts with heuristics. A heuristic is the procedure of finding an adequate, but usually imperfect, answer to a complex question in a simple way. Thus, a complex question is hereby replaced by a simple question. This is efficient, but not always correct.

From the use of heuristics, cognitive biases, thinking errors, can subsequently arise. This involves not applying a logical rule, even though it is clearly relevant in a particular case. Finally, these thinking errors can lead to wrong decisions.

It is not easy to prevent thinking errors, since system 1 works automatically and we are therefore not always aware of possible errors. If there is still evidence of a thinking error, it can be prevented by additional checking by system 2. It is therefore especially good to recognize situations in which thinking errors may occur, so that we become aware of them.

The following section gives 10 examples of heuristics and thinking errors that can play a role in decisions made when trading crypto or NFTs.

Examples psychological thinking errors

Anchoring effect

The anchoring effect is a psychological fallacy that causes us to rely too much on the first piece of information we receive about a subject. When we make a particular judgment, we interpret newer information from the reference point of our "anchor," rather than seeing it objectively. This can distort our judgment and keep us from continually updating our predictions properly.

For example, if you first read information that a new crypto currency will be very successful and will definitely be worth $100, this effect can cause you to take more negative information about the currency - for example, an estimate of a maximum value of only $1 - that you read afterwards less seriously. The number 100 is then used in our minds as a 'comparison anchor' for the estimate we make, while that number does not have to be relevant at all or is even completely out of the blue.

Availability heuristic

The availability heuristic describes our tendency to use examples that come quickly and easily to mind when making decisions about the future. When we can remember something specific, we will give that more weight than newer data, which can lead to misjudging risks and opportunities.

An example of this is if you specifically choose to invest in Bitcoin because you think you can make a lot of profit with it because you've read all over the media that this crypto currency has skyrocketed in recent years. On the other hand, if you had based your choice on a thorough analysis of options, other crypto currencies could have emerged that might allow you to make much more profit because they had even more growth potential than Bitcoin. So in this way, your estimation is influenced and investment opportunities are limited.

Bandwagon effect
The bandwagon effect is a psychological fallacy, where people do something primarily because other people are doing it. Your choices are aligned with what other people are doing and own beliefs are ignored in the process. This is also called herd behavior.

We see this phenomenon for example when people buy crypto coins or NFTs purely because of the hype and FOMO. They then make a purchase without doing any research themselves, hoping to make money quickly. Unfortunately, this often turns out to be wrong, causing losses.

Confirmation bias
Confirmation bias describes our underlying tendency to focus more on and place more value on information that fits our own existing beliefs. In such cases, information that confirms existing opinions is sought

out and data that refutes them is ignored. Decisions are thereby distorted based on our own cognitive biases.

This occurs, for example, when we are very bullish about a particular crypto currency, and we filter out useful negative information that does not match our own ideas. This can lead us to not consider serious risks in decisions.

Ostrich effect

The ostrich effect refers to ignoring negative information when making decisions, by burying one's head in the sand, as it were. This effect is named after the fable about the flight behavior of an ostrich, which would put its head in the sand to avoid seeing the enemy, assuming that the danger would then also be unable to see the ostrich.

We see this reflected in practice in investors' tendency to avoid negative information. For example, one study also found that during bear markets, investors are less likely to look at the value of their investments.

Outcome bias

The outcome bias refers to judging a decision based on the (already known) outcome, without considering the quality of the decision that preceded it and the information that was known beforehand. Thus, the correctness of a decision is judged solely on the basis of the consequences of the decision, and takes into account information that was not previously available.

The fact that you got a positive result does not mean that the decision was right. The danger of this is that you make follow-up decisions based on the positive consequences, and these may turn out to be quite different.

For example, if you invested in a shitcoin because it was hyped and you made a lot of profit, it does not mean that it was a smart decision and that you will make a lot of profit again in the future in this way.

Overconfidence effect
The overconfidence effect means that some people have too much confidence in their own abilities, which causes them to take bigger risks in everyday life.

We see this, for example, in traders who present their own way of trading and strategies as the means to achieve improbable but desired profits, without considering the risks involved.

Pro-innovation bias
The pro-innovation bias involves the tendency of a proponent of an innovative concept to overestimate its usefulness and actually underestimate its limitations or not see them at all.

For example, new crypto or NFT projects are often promoted as innovative, trend-setting and as a new "hype," so investors fail to consider their limitations or weaknesses. The fact that a certain project is innovative does not mean that it is well constructed or that the team is reliable, while these are important points to consider when you want to invest in something.

Survivorship bias
The survivorship bias is a psychological fallacy that arises from focusing only on examples of 'survivors', causing us to misjudge a situation. We then only look at the positive outcomes, which is often only a small percentage of the whole. So the large percentage of negative results are forgotten and not taken into account when making a decision.

For example, you may think that it is easy to make a lot of money with crypto or NFTs, because you often only hear success stories. However, a large proportion also suffer losses.

Zero-risk bias
Zero-risk bias is a psychological fallacy in which we prefer absolute certainty to risk when making decisions, even if it is disadvantageous. In this process, people prefer to eliminate risk completely, while avoiding alternatives with more risk that could lead to better outcomes. This can lead to more negative results, because better results could be achieved if risks were taken.

In other words, risk-taking may yield greater benefits than those obtained when risks are completely avoided. Earlier Elon Musk also pointed this out:

77

There's a tremendous bias against taking risks. Everyone is trying to optimize their ass-covering.

For example, when the bear market entered in early 2018, a lot of panic ensued and many people sold their Bitcoin for fiat to completely hedge risks. However, many people made big losses as a result, whereas if they hadn't sold their crypto coins at that time they would have made a lot of profit now.

This chapter explained why we make wrong choices and gave several examples of psychological thinking errors when trading crypto and NFTs. It is not easy to avoid these errors, because - even if we think we are thinking well - we can still go wrong in predictable ways.

It is therefore especially good to recognize situations in which psychological thinking errors may occur, so that we can become aware of them and can avoid pitfalls in order to make better quality decisions. So be sure to take advantage of this!

Undercollateralized loans

When you want to borrow crypto on a platform set up for that purpose, you often need to secure collateral. This is because there is no middle man, so users must be able to trust each other. However, this does ensure that not everyone can borrow crypto. In most cases, the rich can borrow even more, while the poor fall by the wayside.

Many parties are working on finding solutions. They are doing so by developing new protocols that contribute to the issuance of undercollateralized loans. It is possible for it to take out a crypto loan without having to pay full (or no) collateral.

Below I explain everything you need to know about undercollateralized loans. I also discuss all the categories within "undercollateralized loans" and discuss the protocols that belong to them.

Crypto lending, what about it?
Borrowing and lending crypto is an important part of DeFi (Decentralized Finance). There are many different platforms where you can lend cryptocurrencies to others, or borrow crypto from other people. When you lend crypto, you receive an interest on the lent crypto. This interest is paid by the people who borrow the crypto. They eventually have to pay interest on the borrowing. Within crypto, we call this "Lending.

What are Undercollateralized Loans?
Undercollateralized loans are crypto loans with no collateral or collateral that is lower than the value of the borrowed assets. Normally, you have to hold crypto as collateral before you can take a loan. Since everything works decentrally, this is necessary to build trust. However, it does ensure that not everyone can take out a loan. After all, you only have to hold just enough crypto. This creates a gap between rich and poor.

With undercollateralized loans, it is possible for both rich and poor to borrow cryptocurrency. According to many people, undercollateralized loans are not a replacement for overcollateralized loans. Instead, they address a completely new market that is more widely distributed.

At first glance, it may seem impossible. After all, how do you get people to lend out their crypto when others don't have to put up collateral, or lower collateral, for it? Of course, you don't want someone to not repay your cryptocurrencies. Yet, there are already several protocols that have managed to pull it off.

Which undercollateralized loans protocols are there?
There are several protocols that offer undercollateralized loans. They all do this in a different way, so we can classify these protocols into different categories. Below you can see which categories they are, and which protocols they belong to.

Crypto Native Credit Scores

Crypto native credit scores are ideal for personal loans and microfinance. The idea behind this model is to build an on-chain identity for each user. The history of users is stored, in order to get a better idea about the behavior of users.

This is needed to determine if someone should be considered for a loan. If it turns out that someone has failed to pay (on time) several times in the past, these users can be excluded from future loans. After all, nobody is waiting for defaulters.

This concerns data from historical loans, yield farming, trading activities, participation in governance, etc. At the same time, the privacy of users must be sufficiently guaranteed. Some protocols solve this by using technologies such as Zk proofs. The authorized parties can then only see the results, while other data remains protected.

Crypto native credit scores allow people and protocols to see if someone may qualify for a loan. They then do not have to pay full collateral, so protocols within crypto native credit scores contribute to the development of undercollateralized loans.

These are well-known crypto native credit scores protocols:

LedgerScore (LED);

Credmark (CMK);
EasyFi (EZ);
Wing (WING);
Zoracles (ZORA);
Arc.
Third-Party Risk Assessment.
Third-party risk assessments are ideal for personal loans, microfinance and decentralized prime brokerage. The advantage of this type of loan is that the risk is distributed, leaving users with a much lower risk. This makes it attractive to use third-party risk assessments.

In this model, a third party (not a borrower or lender) called an assessor is chosen to perform a credit assessment. For this they are rewarded, but they will also have to discontinue some assets. Should a default occur, their stake will be taken away first.

This model makes it possible to borrow crypto without having to pay the full collateral. This opens up many possibilities. At the same time, an on-chain credit scoring system is built. Should a user fail to pay their loans, this will be stored. It will then become increasingly easy for credit review parties to reject defaulters.

The biggest disadvantage of this system is in the first months or years. No system of credit scores has been built up by then, making it difficult to assess whether someone may be eligible to take out a loan.

Because users do not have to pay full collateral, third-party risk assessments loans belong to undercollateralized loans.

These are well-known third-party risk assessments protocols:

Goldfinch (GFI);
Dharma;
Maple (MPL);
TrueFi (TRU);
Bloom (BLOOM).
Flash Loans
Flash loans can be used for arbitrage, collateral swaps and liquidity. The advantage is that all parties involved recover their assets almost immediately and the risk involved is small. However, flash loans often cannot be used for personal purposes.

With a flash loan the borrowed assets must be repaid in the same transaction. Thus, this is not convenient when you want to take out a loan for a longer period of time. Instead, flash loans are ideal for traders who want to make use of small price fluctuations between different DEX's in combination with a leverage (margin trading).

Thus, with a flash loan you do not need to secure collateral that is higher than the amount borrowed. That is why flash loans belong to undercollateralized loans.

These are known flash loan protocols:

Aave (AAVE);
Dydx (DYDX);
Equalizer (EQZ).

Personal network bootstrap protocols are ideal for personal loans. Also, the probability of default with these types of protocols is incredibly low. People who want to borrow crypto will first have to be added by members of the lending pool. This means that the platform grows organically, just like a network.

There is a lot of trust between the members of the pool. Everyone knows each other, which makes it easier to keep defaulters out. Yet you would think that it is difficult to keep defaulters out in this way. After all, anyone can add and accept new members. Many protocols have figured this out.

If you have added a defaulter, you could be penalized. Therefore, inviting people you don't know can be an expensive joke. The risk is simply too great.

These are well-known personal network bootstrap protocols:

Acropolis (AKRO)
Union (UNN)
Aave (AAVE)

Real-world Asset Loans
Unlike other protocols, you could use real-world asset loans for, say, a mortgage. In fact, you can use this type of loan for any real-world asset. Quite unique, because the financing is done entirely on the blockchain.

The real-world asset loans are represented as NFTs on the blockchain. The NFTs count in part as collateral for the loan. So you can compare this to mortgages issued by banks. In that type of mortgage, the buildings are also the collateral of the loan.

If the user who has borrowed the money can no longer pay his loan, the money can be paid back with the NFT. These can be resold. The buyer of the NFT then buys the certificate of ownership of the underlying real-world asset.

The biggest challenge is mainly in liquidity and regulation. It is easy to say that a certain NFT represents the proof of ownership of a house, but local laws and regulations have to be in place. In the Netherlands, for example, NFTs are not yet considered legal proof of ownership. Therefore, a lot will have to change before these types of loans can work on a large scale.

These are well-known real-world asset lending protocols:

Centrifuge (CFG)
OpenDAO (SOS)

RealT (REAL)

NFTs as Collateral
There are also protocols where you can use NFT as collateral for a loan. NFTs have become incredibly popular in recent years, and many of these types of tokens have therefore increased in value. It can therefore be attractive to use these tokens for Lending.

Although it is a unique idea, it remains to be seen whether this will work. After all, the value of an NFT is primarily based on hype. The value of NFT-art can quite easily collapse like a house of cards. This makes it difficult to attach a value to the NFTs that are set as collateral.

Nevertheless, we are seeing a growing interest in these types of loans. NFTs are popular, and people prefer to use them for as many purposes as possible.

These are well-known NFTs as collateral protocols:

Helio (HLO)
Lendroid (LST)
Stater (STR)
Aave (AAVE)
YouHodler
NFTfi

Off-chain Credit Integration

For personal loans and microfinance, off-chain credit integration is very useful. This is because these types of protocols have a lot of data from users and can establish connections between other protocols. This makes it easy to find out a lot about certain users.

With off-chain credit integration, data that is on central servers is integrated to the blockchain. There is of course much more data about people available off-chain, than is available on-chain. Banks, insurance companies and other financial institutions track people's behavior. They do this in order to determine whether someone should be allowed to access certain services.

If it turns out that someone never pays their taxes and premiums on time, a landlord could bar someone. The chance that the potential tenant will not pay his rent on time is then too high.

By moving this kind of data to the blockchain, it is easier to determine whether someone should be allowed to get a crypto loan. People who turn out to be creditworthy then don't have to put up any collateral, or substantially less.

These are well-known off-chain credit integration protocols:

Counter (TELLER)

Digital Asset Loans
Digital asset loans protocols are ideal for leveraged
trading. As a result, these types of protocols are very
similar to flash loans. The difference, however, is that
the purchased assets are placed in a smart contact until
the loan is paid off. If the trade does not go well, the
contract can liquidate the position after which the loss
is covered by the protocol. Then the full amount is paid
back to the lender. So the lender does not have to
worry about repayment.

These are well-known digital asset lending protocols:

Lendefi (LDFI)

With undercollateralized loans it is a lot easier to
borrow crypto. You don't have to put up any (or much
less) collateral. There are several categories within
undercollateralized loans. There are a total of dozens of
protocols that belong to them, the most important of
which you have read above.

On-chain analysis

If you are going to invest in the crypto market, you can benefit a lot from on-chain analysis. In this chapter, I'll take you through what on-chain data analysis is, how to apply it and what indicators you can use.

What is blockchain?
Blockchain technology is playing an increasingly important role in our lives, even though it is still abracadabra for many people.

Blockchain is a database with a chain of blocks. The blocks contain approved transactions, with all kinds of new transactions, new blocks are added to the chain.

Because the blocks are approved by other users, the margin of error is extremely small. Once executed transactions cannot be reversed, increasing security.

Blockchain vs. Crypto
You now know a little bit about what blockchain is all about, but what does it have to do with cryptocurrencies? Trading with money requires a high degree of security, which was not fully covered in the early versions of blockchain. At the time, you could just spend your digital coins twice, which of course is not the intention.

A stable financial system needs a secure foundation and transparency. By tracking data, showing where transactions are made, and by whom, you can remove the central intermediary from the process. And that's how the blockchain made it possible to trade in cryptocurrencies.

A blockchain is really nothing more than a collection of transactions, with the actions recorded in the blocks. Security is ensured through hashes, which come from the Secure Hashing Algorithm.

For the doubters and those who have doubts about a digital financial system, maybe these great investors will change your mind.

What is on-chain analysis?
You are now aware of some basic knowledge, such as what is the blockchain and how can a digital money system work based on this technology. But at what point is it best to get in, are the prices predictable? What causes prices to rise or fall?

Technical analysis studies the price action, fundamental analysis looks at the influence of external factors on the currency. But what does on-chain analysis do? On-chain analysis focuses on analyzing the data on the blockchain, so you can understand the elements that influence the price action.

With this data you can better assess what the price of the digital currency will do, so you can better respond to it. We also call this determining the market sentiment.

Do realize that trading in crypto is always risky, just like trading in stocks. By performing analyses you do get a better idea of the economic state of being, the value of the coin and the potential outcome. In this chapter I will dive deeper into performing on-chain analysis, do you read along?

On-chain analysis indicators
Okay, you know the definition now, but now we're really going to take a deeper dive. There are multiple indicators, but they ultimately boil down to two key metrics: the number of active user addresses and an increase or decrease in the number of transactions.

Let's start with some analysis indicators, as they indicate who is active in the crypto market and what kind of actions they are taking. These are three popular indicators, which are also great to analyze with a tool, such as Glassnode:

- CDD - Coin Days Destroyed
- SOPR - Spent Output Profit Ratio
- SOAB - Spent Output Age Bands

Besides these three on-chain indicators, you have many others, such as realized profit/loss, unrealized profit/loss, stablecoin, liveliness, ASOL, NVT, etc.

Coin Days Destroyed

This is a measure you use to calculate, when the last transaction of a coin took place. The longer a coin is on inactive, the more heavily this factor weighs. So each day that a coin is not deployed on the market counts for one coin day.

Why is this important to know? Because if a relatively large number of digital coins are being traded, then something is going on in the market. This can be positive or negative, but something is going on. If the price is rising and the CDD is rising, you can expect HODL players to want to take advantage and hand in their coins for a hefty profit.

If there is a rising market, but little change in the CDD, then this is a signal for a bullish market. It means that investors are choosing to hold on to their currency, so they are confident in their choice.

Finally, you have the sideways trend, which is when there are no price fluctuations and the market is quite stable. Are investors going to redeem the coins - so the CDD rises - then they have lost their enthusiasm and will look for a more attractive investment.

Calculation of the CDD Incator

The calculation of the CDD indicator value is as follows: the number of coins issued x the lifetime of these coins. An example: 3 BTC that have been on inactive for 100 days have collectively accumulated 300 coin days.

Spent Output Profit Ratio

The second indicator we are going to cover is the SOPR. This represents all the losses and gains of coins that are repositioned on on-chain. It is tied to the macro market segment, thanks to its representation of profitability and losses incurred, within a certain period of time.

You measure this indicator by measuring the coins, which have moved in the time period. This can be in an hour, day or week, just to name a few. You look specifically at the fiat value at the time of UTXO creation as well as the value of the UTXO when it is issued. The UTXO is the unspent transaction output.

Calculation of the SOPR indicator

The calculation of this indicator is as follows: divide the realized value of the output in USD by the value at creation of the original UTXO in USD. Several outcomes are possible:

SOPR > 1 - the sale price is higher than the purchase price
SOPR < 1 - the sale price is lower than the purchase price
SOPR = 1 - the coins are sold at break even
SORP higher trend represents gains and the return of illiquid coins to circulation
SORP lower trend represents losses and/or that profitable coins are not issued.

Spent Output Age Bands

This SOAB indicator is a metric that classifies already issued coins into categories, based on age and color bands them as a percentage of the total number of coins moved.

By being aware of the Spent Output Age Bands, you can assess if there are periods, where transactions are dominated by younger or older coins. This means that you can intelligently see if the market movements are influenced by HODL'ers or by the newer participants in the crypto market.

Cooler colors prevail, when most of the trading involves old coins. If younger coins in particular are active, then you get a warmer picture. You can specify the analysis by turning legend items on or off in Glassnode.

Calculation SOAB

The calculation of SOAB is done as follows: first you calculate the age of the coins that are issued within a certain period of time, such as an hour. Then you're going to see how this number compares to the total number of coins spent, so you have a percentage at hand. You can select a whole slew of time periods, including: <1 hour, 1-24 hours, weeks, months, quarters, years up to and including >10 years.

What is Glassnode?

Now that we know a bit more about on-chain indicators, and I've already brought Glassnode into it a few times, I want to introduce you to the power of this on-chain data and intelligence platform. This provider gives you access to all the on-chain data for you, because you can access the numbers from all kinds of different blockchains.

Glassnode's newsletter is completely free, keeping you up to date with the state of the crypto market on a weekly basis with useful figures and cool videos. If you really want to make something of your trading on the blockchain, a paid subscription is a better idea.

The benefits of this tool:

- Large number of metrics
- Many assets supporting
- Accurate data on-chain
- Easy to apply

How do you apply on-chain analysis?
All data on the blockchain, but also on cryptocurrencies, is completely transparent, which enables you to extensively analyze which way the market is moving. This gives you insight into the reason for the price rise or fall. Use the tooling cleverly and do not assume that it will effortlessly solve all your problems, because that is obviously not what it is intended for.

Of course, it is also a pretty logical picture, because if there is no movement in the market and many addresses and coins are inactive, then it is a sideways, stable market. If, through your analysis, you see the number of active addresses and the number of transactions in cryptocurrencies increasing, then you can wait and see that something is going on. There is increasing demand, which often causes prices to rise as well.

Alternative sources for crypto analysis?
Besides Glassnode, you can also follow news stories, such as through Twitter.

These are some accounts that have a lot to say about charts, on-chain metrics and other analytical matters:

- @100trillionUSD - "All models are wrong, but some are useful"
- @woonomic - "#Bitcoin analyst"
- @chartsBtc - "A bitcoiner with a spreadsheet"
- @CaitlinLong_ - "Founder/CEO @Custodiabank. 22-yr Wall St veteran"
- @pierre_rochard - "Product @KrakenFX, advisor @RiotBlockchain."
- @Rhythmtrader - "#Bitcoin"
- @finhamsterdam - "Payments and digital money regulation/compliance expert"

Although on-chain analysis provides a lot of valuable information, allowing you to make better decisions about your trading ability, it is not the solution for big profits. You'll really need your knowledge, experience and common sense to come to a reliable judgment.

With this kind of analysis you'll get insight in the market movement and you'll know why price rises and falls take place. This is valuable, because you can use this information in your decision to buy or sell digital coins.

Derivatives

Investors often have a diversified portfolio, which comes in shapes and sizes. Derivatives are investment instruments, which track an underlying asset. You can enter into a contract that focuses on commodities, a particular currency or an index.

In this chapterm I'll take you through the definition of derivatives, how to trade in them and what the risks are. Once the basics are covered, we'll also dive into crypto derivatives, because that's what you came here for. Right?

What are derivatives?
You'd be surprised how often people google what exactly the meaning of derivatives is. In fact, literally, derivative means nothing more than derivative, but of course this hardly says anything, so let's dive in a little further.

Options, futures and swaps are all investment instruments, which we also call derivatives. These derivatives follow an underlying asset, such as commodities, stocks or currencies are. If the prices of the relevant value rise, then the prices of the derivative also rise, and vice versa.

Derivatives are designed to reduce risk for the buyer, because by buying a derivative you have the right to buy or sell something for a certain price.

The history of derivatives
The origins of these investment instruments lie
somewhere in the 16th century, when farmers wanted
to hedge the risks of their agricultural products. In the
Middle Ages, there was a super famous derivatives
market: the Amsterdam tulip exchange.

A tulip farmer wanted to be assured of the sale of his
bulbs, so that bad harvests or price drops would not
cause him suffering. He entered into an agreement with
a trader, in which a price was agreed upon. Of course,
this was something of a risk to both parties, because the
price was lower than the farmer could charge in the
event of a good harvest, but higher than he would
capture in the event of a crop failure.

This price fixing is called a derivative, since the
underlying asset was a tulip crop. The farmer cleverly
reduced his risk by making an attractive deal.

The great tulip craze
The fall of 1636 saw a major drama unfold in one of
Amsterdam's wealthiest merchant houses, according to
wikipedia. Passersby saw staff of the wealthy lord
running back and forth, turning everything upside
down. They were looking for a tulip bulb.

You might be thinking now, a tulip bulb? Why all the
drama over a flower, but this bulb had the value of 3000
guilders. This is equivalent to over € 600,000 in today's

society, so you can imagine what a misery that must have been.

The tulip became a status symbol and object of speculation.

Experienced investors made smart use of price fluctuations, because by speculating you can make a contract many times more lucrative. The tulip frenzy in the Dutch Republic is a textbook example of this!

How do derivatives work?
Derivatives can deliver large profits, but can also plunge deep into the red.

How is this possible?
Because of the leverage effect. Suppose you conclude an agreement for a certain price, because you expect this price to rise. If the prices do not subsequently rise, but instead fall. Then you have caused yourself some pain, because that is what you feel in the papers.

How can you invest in derivatives?
Derivatives can be traded in various ways, namely via the stock exchange or mutually. This mutual trading, outside the stock exchange, is also called OTC: over the counter.

Thanks to the standardized contracts, trading is easy and liquidity is high, which is attractive for the investor.

I think it is useful to first go through the different types of derivatives, so you know what to look out for. In our financial system, derivatives have become indispensable in the stock market, so pay attention!

Different types of derivatives
Derivatives come in all shapes and sizes, but are certainly not for the novice on the investment market.

There are turbos, speeders, boosters and sprinters, but also call and put options, binary options, CFDs, warrants and much more.

In this chapter we will only cover the most well-known types of derivatives, namely:
- Options
- CFDs
- Futures
- Swaps
- Options

An option is a financial product. It gives the buyer of this product the right to buy or sell an underlying asset at a set price. This is similar to the story of the Amsterdam tulip farmer, as I described above.

When buying such a derivative, an expiration date is immediately set, so a kind of deadline. The underlying asset can be a stock, commodity or certain index and the value of the option is therefore based on the price of this underlying asset.

101

CFDs

Investing in CFDs is becoming increasingly popular. CFD stands for Contract For Difference. The contract is concluded between the broker and the investor and, unlike other options, does not entitle you to own the underlying asset. If the price goes up, you are entitled to a profit distribution and if the price goes down, you are obliged to pay.

What you are actually doing with CFDs is speculating on a price rise or price fall, by means of a lever.

Futures

A future is a forward contract, whereby buyer and seller enter into an agreement. This agreement contains a time and a price, at which the underlying financial product is transferred. It is therefore a serious commitment that you should not enter into without knowledge and experience.

You buy futures for commodities, such as gold, silver and oil. You can also put your money in government bonds and stock indices, it just depends on what you see value in.

Swaps

Swaps are financial products in which two parties exchange something. You might be thinking, huh? Are the flippos back from the past, but no, we are talking about exchanging interest payments.

A derivative is used to hedge interest rate risk or take a particular position. The value depends on the interest rate during the swap, so you can imagine that this is a very time-sensitive investment.

Crypto derivatives
After this very long introduction, where I buried you in a lot of knowledge, I'm now going to tell you a bit about crypto derivatives. I already told you above that derivatives follow an underlying asset, such as a commodity or currency. This currency does not have to be the USD, but can also be a cryptocurrency.

The crypto market is growing by giant leaps every day, which also attracts the attention of derivatives investors. Crypto derivatives open a new world for investors, because of their flexibility and ease of trading.

You can buy these derivatives both on the exchange and over the counter (OTC). The very first crypto derivative was launched in 2012 on the Bitcoin forum. The initiator was a broker named Satoshi Option, but this ended in a hiss.

Subsequently, several products were launched in 2017, which did turn out to be sustainable. LedgerX was the first to successfully trade Bitcoin Derivatives. They traded over $1 million on the exchange in the first week.

DeFi Derivatives

While we're on the digital scene, let's also touch on derivatives in the world of DeFi. DeFi stands for Decentralized Finance, which in my opinion is the future of our financial system.

Enthusiasts are convinced that these DeFi derivatives have even more advantages, than any other form of investing. The best smart contracts come to mind, but what else is so special about these investment tools within the world of DeFi?

Risks of trading derivatives.

You may be opening your wallet right now, to invest in derivatives, but are you aware of the risks? After all, it's not all sunshine and roses hey! These are the biggest risks, which you as an investor should be aware of:

Due to leverage, you can see huge differences in your invested capital. A small fluctuation in the price can have a big impact on your assets through leverage.

Particularly in the crypto scene, this is of course watchful, because of the volatility. In many cases, your losses can be unlimited, which can leave you deeply in debt;

The value of derivatives are based on what the market does. As a result, the contracts follow the price, but are just empty of content. If the market collapses, as it just does once in a while, the derivative positions plummet like crazy. If you want to know more about economic cycles, I can heartily recommend the books and content of Ray Dalio. Very informative!
Derivatives are enormously complex financial products, so as a beginner, make sure you don't just jump in blindly. Be well informed, read up and only trade when you have gained enough knowledge!
High costs when trading derivatives. If you invest in a stock through DEGIRO or you buy some digital coins through Bitvavo, the costs are often zero. With derivatives this is different. Depending on the type of derivatives you agree on, the costs can be quite high.

As you could have read in this chapter, investing in derivatives is a complex matter. There are quite a few risks, which you cannot and do not want to take for granted. There are various types of derivatives, which you can purchase in two different ways. I've taken you through the development of these investment instruments up to the present day, so that you have a good insight into the developments in the financial sector.

In addition to the standard derivatives, you also have fairly new derivatives, namely crypto and DeFi agreements. These stick together slightly differently, but carry just as much risk. Of course, investing is always risky, but derivatives are really for the serious, experienced investor.

Your FREE book

If you want to make a profitable start in the world of cryptocurrency, make sure to download our free bonus with **12 extremely valuable tips for beginners!**

With this book and these tips, you're guaranteed to make a great start with your future investments!

Sign up here to get instant access and kickstart your crypto success:

https://campsite.bio/stellarmoonpublishing

Our Crypto Expert Trading Course

Are you looking for a new way to invest?

Are you looking to make some money?

Interested in investing but do not know where to start?

Do you want to start your crypto trading with the knowledge of reputable experts in finance and investment?

The crypto Expert Trading Course is the most comprehensive course on trading and investing with cryptocurrencies. You will learn how to trade in just a few minutes per day. We teach you everything from technical analysis, risk management, and much more.

Our goal is to help you become a successful trader so that your financial future can be secure.

Investing has never been easier with our step-by-step blueprint that teaches beginners how to trade like an expert – with the potential of making huge profits!

The best part about this course is taught by experts. So, what are you waiting for? Start today!

For more information, visit this link:

https://payhip.com/b/ork8N

www.ingramcontent.com/pod-product-compliance
Lightning Source LLC
Chambersburg PA
CBHW061242140726
47998CB00006B/2067